I0415823

Establishment of Survey Sites for Monitoring Landbirds within the Klamath Network

Natural Resource Data Series NPS/KLMN/NRDS—2010/126

Jaime L. Stephens

Klamath Bird Observatory
PO Box 758
Ashland, OR 97520

John D. Alexander

Klamath Bird Observatory
PO Box 758
Ashland, OR 97520

Sean R. Mohren

Klamath Inventory and Monitoring Network
1250 Siskiyou Blvd.
Ashland, OR 97520

December 2010

U.S. Department of the Interior
National Park Service
Natural Resource Program Center
Fort Collins, Colorado

The National Park Service, Natural Resource Program Center publishes a range of reports that address natural resource topics of interest and applicability to a broad audience in the National Park Service and others in natural resource management, including scientists, conservation and environmental constituencies, and the public.

The Natural Resource Data Series is intended for timely release of basic data sets and data summaries. Care has been taken to assure accuracy of raw data values, but a thorough analysis and interpretation of the data has not been completed. Consequently, the initial analyses of data in this report are provisional and subject to change.

All manuscripts in the series receive the appropriate level of peer review to ensure that the information is scientifically credible, technically accurate, appropriately written for the intended audience, and designed and published in a professional manner. Data in this report were collected and analyzed using methods based on established, peer-reviewed protocols and were analyzed and interpreted within the guidelines of the protocols.

Views, statements, findings, conclusions, recommendations, and data in this report do not necessarily reflect views and policies of the National Park Service, U.S. Department of the Interior. Mention of trade names or commercial products does not constitute endorsement or recommendation for use by the U.S. Government.

This report is available from the Klamath Network website (http://science.nature.nps.gov/im/units/klmn/Monitoring/vs/Landbird/VS_Landbirds.cfm) and the Natural Resource Publications Management website (http://www.nature.nps.gov/publications/NRPM).

Please cite this publication as:

Stephens, J. L., J. D. Alexander, and S.R. Mohren. 2010. Establishment of survey sites for monitoring landbirds within the Klamath Network. Natural Resource Data Series NPS/KLMN/NRDS—2010/126. National Park Service, Fort Collins, Colorado.

NPS 963/106308, Month Year

Contents

Figures

Tables

Abstract

From 2007 through 2010, Klamath Bird Observatory, in partnership with the Klamath Inventory and Monitoring Network (KLMN) of the National Park Service, completed the establishment of survey sites for the Klamath Network: Landbird Monitoring Protocol. Landbird monitoring contributes to the vital signs monitoring program that has been developed by the KLMN. A landbird monitoring protocol was designed to yield important information about avian community composition, status of landbirds in a given year, and long-term population trends for each KLMN park unit. For the establishment of point count routes, the sampling frame and corresponding populations being sampled were selected based on a variety of criteria. Criteria included accessibility, safety and minimal disturbance, co-location with other KLMN monitoring protocols, and presence of Oregon/Washington and California Partners in Flight (PIF) focal bird species, continental PIF bird species of concern, Oregon Department of Fish and Wildlife conservation strategy bird species, and California conservation strategy bird species and/or to address park priorities. This report provides an overview of the study design and sampling frame selection, outlines the process of site development using ArcGIS, and describes the process of monumenting sites in the field.

Acknowledgments

We thank Daniel Sarr at the Klamath Network and the park biologists for their contributions to the Landbird Monitoring Protocol. Establishment of sampling locations would not have been possible without the help of the park staff. Special thanks to Barbara Alberti, Mac Brock, Jennifer Gibson, Terri Hines, David Hays, Gregory Holm, David Larson, Michael Magnuson, Steve Mark, John McClelland, Sue Mclaughlin, Scott Powell, Jim Richardson, John Roth, Kristin Schmidt, Brett Silver, Amber Transou, Judy Wartella, and Russ Weatherbee for their logistical support. The dedication of the field technicians has made this project successful. Field technicians whom contributed to establishment of point count survey sites included Jim DeStaebler, Lyndia Hammer, Jherime Kellerman, and Frank Lospalluto. Additional thanks to Lorin Groshong, Jennifer Bruce, and Danielle Morris for their GIS contributions to this project and report. Elizabeth (Bess) Perry's help in editing this report was also much appreciated.

Introduction

In 2010, Klamath Bird Observatory, in partnership with the Klamath Inventory and Monitoring Network (KLMN) of the National Park Service, completed the establishment of survey sites for the Klamath Network: Landbird Monitoring Protocol (Stephens et al. 2010). This report provides an overview of site establishment, including (1) a summary of the monitoring protocol, (2) a description of the study design and sampling frames, and (3) a summary of monumenting activities at each park.

The KLMN, located in southern Oregon and northern California, includes Crater Lake National Park (CRLA), Lassen Volcanic National Park (LAVO), Lava Beds National Monument (LABE), Oregon Caves National Monument (ORCA), Redwood National and State Parks (RNSP), and Whiskeytown National Recreation Area (WHIS). These park units fall within the Klamath Region. This region includes a broad range of topography, elevation, and corresponding climate and vegetation. The region is recognized for its rich biodiversity, which is represented by diverse avifauna (DellaSala et al. 1999, Trail et al. 1997).

Landbird monitoring contributes to the vital signs monitoring program that has been developed by the KLMN (Sarr et al. 2007). A landbird monitoring protocol was designed to yield important information about avian community composition, status of landbirds in a given year, and long-term population trends for each KLMN park unit (Stephens et al. 2010). The avian sampling methods incorporated in this protocol include point count surveys, constant effort mist netting, area search surveys, and a compilation of species checklists at specific sites. The methodology selected for each park was based on park unit size, habitat composition, and historic bird monitoring efforts (Stephens et al. 2010).

The KLMN landbird monitoring effort is informed by and contributes to regional and continental bird monitoring programs including, among others, the Partners in Flight (PIF) landbird conservation initiative. In addition, KLMN landbird monitoring is integrated with an extensive regional bird monitoring network known as the Klamath Bird Monitoring Network (Frey et al. 2010, Stephens and Alexander 2010). The Klamath Bird Monitoring Network is a bird monitoring partnership that extends across the Klamath-Siskiyou Bioregion (Alexander et al. 2004), coordinated by the Klamath Bird Observatory and U.S. Forest Service Redwood Sciences Laboratory.

The objectives of the Klamath Network Landbird Monitoring Protocol are to:
1) Monitor breeding landbird richness, relative abundance, and density.
2) Co-sample habitat parameters and integrate bird and vegetation monitoring to aid in interpretation of landbird status and trends.
3) Determine status and trends in demographic parameters (productivity, adult survival, and recruitment) for selected landbird species in a mixed-conifer and riparian habitat at Oregon Caves National Monument.

This report provides an overview of study design and sampling frame selection, which are further detailed in the Klamath Network: Landbird Monitoring Protocol (Stephens et al. 2010).

In addition, this report outlines the process of site establishment using ArcGIS and the monumenting of sites in the field.

Methods

Sampling Design

The KLMN Landbird Monitoring Protocol incorporates multiple standard avian sampling methods (Ralph et al. 1993, Stephens et al. 2010), including variable circular plot point counts, constant effort mist netting, area search surveys, species checklists, and habitat surveys. The use of these complementary methods, which gather information about multiple bird species, will optimize the amount of information gathered about birds in each park. Twenty five to 35 point count routes were established at each park unit corresponding to park unit size, with the exception of Oregon Caves National Monument. Due to the relatively small size of the monument, monitoring at this park includes a constant effort mist net station and four point count routes.

Sampling Frame

The ORCA constant effort monitoring station is a Sentinel site. Sentinel sites are defined as locations of special interest to sample, or where historical monitoring efforts warrant continuity in sampling. They are selected subjectively on the basis of being representative of a particular habitat or environment of interest and accessibility. The ORCA constant effort monitoring station is characteristic of the mixed-conifer and riparian habitats within the park.

For the establishment of point count routes, the sampling frame and corresponding populations being sampled were selected based on a variety of criteria. Criteria included logistical, safety, statistical and funding constraints, as well as co-location with sites associated with other KLMN monitoring protocols. One criterion was specific to accessibility; route starting points must be greater than 100 m and less than 1000 m from a road or trail, with exceptions at ORCA and WHIS. At ORCA the sampling frame included locations between 100 m and 1000 m from a road or trail within the proposed expansion area, and within the existing monument the sampling frame included locations between 100 m and 1000 m from a road and within 1000 m of a trail (i.e. location could be established within 100 m of a trail). Because of the high density of trails, this sampling frame was necessary in order to place a point count route within the existing monument. At WHIS the sampling frame was limited to roads, trails, and power lines for safety reasons. Secondly, both for safety concerns and to avoid damage to understory vegetation, we excluded areas having a slope in excess of 30 degrees, talus slopes, and lava flows (Sarr et al. 2007). In addition, in an effort to integrate the data collected as part of the KLMN Vegetation and Aquatic Monitoring Protocols, it is planned to have all landbird routes co-located with sites selected as part of the vegetation and water quality monitoring efforts when applicable. By collocating sites, it is our intent to show that relationships between status and trend patterns can be observed between protocols providing us with a better understanding of the dynamic nature and condition of our park ecosystems (Sarr et al. 2007)

Three potential sampling frames were further delineated and considered for sampling in each park, as appropriate. These delineations included high elevation areas (only in CRLA, LAVO, and WHIS), riparian areas (perennial streams, lakes, ponds, and springs), and matrix areas (everything that was not captured in the high elevation or riparian sampling frames) (Sarr et al. 2007). Sampling frames were selected to maximize the inclusion of Oregon/Washington and California Partners in Flight (PIF) focal bird species (Altman 1999, 2000, CalPIF 2002a, 2002b,

2004, 2005, RHJV 2004), continental PIF bird species of concern (Rich et al. 2004), Oregon Department of Fish and Wildlife conservation strategy bird species (ODFW 2005), and California conservation strategy bird species (CDFG 2005) and/or to address park priorities (Stephens et al. 2010). At LABE, ORCA, and RNSP we selected the matrix sampling frame for establishing landbird monitoring sites. The riparian sampling frame was selected for landbird monitoring sites at LAVO. At CRLA we exclude riparian areas and monitoring sites were established in the matrix and high elevation sampling frames. The sampling frame was limited to roads, trails, and power lines at WHIS, which cover the majority of the park and allow us to sample the matrix areas throughout the elevation range of the park. Maps of each sampling frame are in Appendix A.

Selecting Sampling Locations in ArcGIS

For choosing sampling locations, we used an algorithm termed the Generalized Random Tessellation Stratified (GRTS) method (Stevens and Olsen 2003, 2004) to develop spatially balanced sampling locations within each selected sampling frame for each park. These sampling locations were established for use in the KLMN Vegetation and Aquatic Monitoring Protocols . In order to co-locate the bird survey sites with monitoring sites associated with other KLMN protocols, we selected the previously established GRTS point as one site along a point count route, and developed the remainder of the route around that site.

To establish a systematic random sampling route around each GRTS point, 11 adjacent sites were placed 250 m apart, according to a set of rules (Appendix B). The rules ensure that a route is set up as closely around the GRTS sample as possible, using a systematic, random approach within the constraints used to define the sampling frame. In matrix sampling frames the rules enforce that the route forms a block (LABE, ORCA, RNSP, CRLA), whereas along roads/trails/power lines (WHIS) and streams (LAVO) the routes are linear.

The riparian sampling frame at LAVO included both streams and wetlands. Point count routes along the streams were established according to the linear rule set, but point count routes within wetland areas were established using additional criteria. We used ArcGIS to establish a wetland sampling frame by designating wetland complexes based on the National Wetland Inventory (NWI) data. To create these wetland complexes, the criteria for developing the sampling frame described above were applied to ensure sites would be safe and accessible. Once this was done, all remaining wetlands were buffered using a 150 m buffer. Next, all buffered areas that overlapped were merged together to create a wetland complex. Wetland complexes are not stands of pure wetland. Instead they contain a variety of habitat types including conifer stands, grasslands, and wetlands; however they are predominately composed of wetland habitats. Once the complexes were developed, we used the GRTS method to place spatially balanced survey points throughout all the wetland complexes. Lastly, we established survey points around the selected GRTS points using an aerial photo to best locate a point in wetland habitat but not in a wetland itself.

In addition to establishing 12 points along a point count route, in most cases 3 oversample points were established. These points were created for use in the field and were incorporated into the route if one of the original 12 points needed to be dropped for safety reasons. Oversamples were not created in WHIS or in some instances for LAVO due to spatial limitations; i.e. the oversamples did not fit within the sampling frame. However, oversamples were not needed in any instance in which they were not available.

Establishing Sampling Locations in the Field

From 2007 to 2010, KBO worked with the KLMN to permanently monument sites along each of the point count routes which will be surveyed in accord with the Klamath Network: Landbird Monitoring Protocol (Stephens et al. 2010). Field Technicians used a Garmin GPS unit, along with map and compass, for navigation in the field and used a Trimble GeoXT handheld to determine the exact location of a survey site. Site establishment in matrix and alpine sampling frames (CRLA, ORCA, LABE, RNSP), as well as along roads, trails, and power lines (WHIS) was straightforward. If a site along a route was not accessible due to safety constraints, it was dropped from the route and a pre-defined oversample was established.

At LAVO, site establishment within the riparian sampling frame (streams and wetlands) presented additional logistical challenges. Sites were established in early July, shortly after predicted future survey dates, to best predict water levels. Field Technicians used a Garmin GPS unit and Trimble unit in a similar manner, but when arriving at the site they had the option to re-locate it if necessary to reduce noise and/or move it out of standing water. When establishing sites along a stream, if birds could not be detected by song or call within 50 m due to excessive stream noise, the site was moved perpendicularly away from the stream as needed to reduce noise. In wetland areas, points were adjusted as needed to fall in riparian areas but outside of standing water.

Monumenting Sampling Locations

Sites along the route were monumented in a variety of ways, depending on the park. At CRLA, ORCA, LABE, and RNSP point count survey sites were marked with 5"x5" yellow signs printed with the phrase "This site is part of the long-term landbird monitoring project being conducted by the NPS-Klamath Network Inventory and Monitoring Program" and site name and route number were written using a permanent paint marker (referred to hereafter as large tag) (Figure 1). At WHIS and LAVO, sites were marked with a small 1-inch brass tags with "KLMN" and the point count site number engraved on them (referred to hereafter as small tag) (Figure 2). In addition to one of the markers, in some cases flagging was used to make the site more visible. A GPS coordinate, directions, and site characteristics were recorded for each site along a route (Appendix I in Stephens et al. 2010).

Figure 1. Yellow 5" x 5" metal signs were used to monument permanent point count survey locations at Crater Lake National Park, Lava Beds National Monument, Oregon Caves National Monument, and Redwood National and State Parks.

Figure 2. One inch round brass tags were used to monument permanent point count survey locations at Whiskeytown National Recreation Area and Lassen Volcanic National Park

Crater Lake National Park

In 2009, we established 35 permanent point count survey routes at Crater Lake National Park, each containing 12 survey sites (Appendix C). Each site was monumented with a large tag nailed to a tree. In areas that lacked vegetation, i.e. the alpine sites, survey points were visited to determine accessibility but no permanent marking was established.

Lava Beds National Monument

In 2008, 25 permanent point count survey routes were established at Lava Beds National Monument, each containing 12 survey sites (Appendix C). Each site was monumented with a large tag affixed to either the bole of a tree or attached with wire to a shrub. In addition, pink flagging was hung in areas of thick vegetation, but overall use of flagging was minimized.

Lassen Volcanic National Park

During the summer of 2009 we established 25 permanent point count survey routes at Lassen Volcanic National Monument, each containing 12 survey sites (Appendix C). Each site was monumented with a small tag nailed to the bole of a tree. In addition, a digital photo was taken of each survey point.

Oregon Caves National Monument

In 2010, we established four permanent point count survey routes at Oregon Caves National Monument, each containing 12 survey sites (Appendix C). One survey route was established within the existing monument, and three were established within the proposed expansion area. This area is currently managed by the USDA Forest Service Wild Rivers Ranger District. Each survey site was monumented with a large tag affixed to the bole of a tree. In addition, orange/white striped flagging was hung at sites within the proposed expansion, but no flagging was hung within the existing monument.

Redwood National and State Parks

Thirty permanent point count survey routes were established at Redwood National and State Parks in 2007 and 2008 (Appendix C). Each survey site was monumented with a large tag affixed to the bole of a tree. In addition, pink flagging was hung at sites within the national park and red/white stripe flagging was hung at sites within the state park. The number of points varied between four and nine for each route due to the rugged terrain and thick vegetation at this park complex; most routes consisted of six survey sites (Table 1). During the next survey implementation at RNSP we will consider adding an additional two sites to RW02 if at all possible, resulting in all routes containing a minimum of 6 sites.

Whiskeytown National Recreation Area

In 2009, we established and surveyed 30 permanent point count survey routes at Whiskeytown National Recreation Area, each consisting of 12 survey sites (Appendix C). Sites were monumented using small tags affixed to the bole of a tree.

Table 1. Long-term landbird monitoring sites established at Redwood National and State Parks and the number of points at each site.

Site Code	Site Name	Survey Points
RW01	Redwoods 01	6
RW02	Redwoods 02	4
RW03	Redwoods 03	6
RW04	Redwoods 04	8
RW05	Redwoods 05	6
RW06	Redwoods 06	6
RW07	Redwoods 07	6
RW08	Redwoods 08	6
RW09	Redwoods 09	6
RW10	Redwoods 10	6
RW11	Redwoods 11	6
RW12	Redwoods 12	6
RW13	Redwoods 13	8
RW14	Redwoods 14	6
RW15	Redwoods 15	6
RW16	Redwoods 16	7
RW17	Redwoods 17	8
RW18	Redwoods 18	6
RW19	Redwoods 19	6
RW20	Redwoods 20	6
RW21	Redwoods 21	9
RW22	Redwoods 22	6
RW23	Redwoods 23	6
RW24	Redwoods 24	8
RW25	Redwoods 25	6
RW26	Redwoods 26	6
RW27	Redwoods 27	6
RW28	Redwoods 28	8
RW29	Redwoods 29	6
RW30	Redwoods 30	6
Total		192

Conclusion

Klamath Bird Observatory in partnership with the Klamath Inventory and Monitoring Network (KLMN) of the National Park Service has completed the establishment of survey sites for the Klamath Network: Landbird Monitoring Protocol. The rigorous study design developed in the monitoring protocol and corresponding site selection using ArcGIS contributed to successful site establishment in the field. While site establishment methods varied by park unit, all point count routes have been ground-truthed and described according to various permit requirements. The process of permanently monumented survey sites will assure the successful implementation of the Klamath Network: Landbird Monitoring Protocol into the future.

Lessons Learned

This effort was one of the first KLMN monitoring projects requiring the monumenting of sites that will continue to be revisited for the foreseeable future. In implementing this effort at the six parks, several adjustments had to be made to sampling aspects of the protocol and its implementation schedule including 1) dropping sites because roads and trails shown on the GIS layers no longer exist, 2) adjusting the sample size at RNSP due to rugged terrain and thick vegetation, 3) changing the sampling frame at WHIS due to safety concerns, and 4) sampling LAVO a year later than expected due to logistical hurdles. Making efforts to monument these sites while developing the draft protocol has allowed us the opportunity to save a considerable amount of time and stress that would have occurred if we tried to monument these sites while implementing the final protocol. For future protocols, we recommend the following:

1. Make sure you have the most up-to-date GIS layers to be used in site selection.
2. If funding is available, monument the permanent sites prior to implementing the final protocol.
3. If sites are to be monumented while implementing the protocol be certain to allocate plenty of extra time to make adjustments as needed.
4. Long before starting the monumenting, sit down with the staff at each park (Resource Chiefs, Resource Specialist, etc.) and review the sampling frame, locations of the sites, and methods of monumenting the site. We have found leaving one person out of the loop (such as law enforcement) on these discussions can cause delays in completing the field work.
5. Keep in mind several preselected sites were dropped from the landbird monitoring project because of accessibility issues. This will need to be taken into account when monumenting the sites for the vegetation community monitoring and water quality and aquatic communities monitoring projects to ensure the sites for these projects are co-located.

Literature Cited

Alexander, J. D., C. J. Ralph, K. Hollinger, and B. Hogoboom. 2004. Using a wide-scale landbird monitoring network to determine landbird distribution and productivity in the Klamath Bioregion. Pages 33-41 *in* K. L. Mergenthaler, J. E. Williams, and E. S. Jules, editors. Proceedings of the second conference on Klamath-Siskiyou ecology. Siskiyou Field Institute, Cave Junction, Oregon.

Altman, B. 1999. Conservation strategy for landbirds in coniferous forests of western Oregon and Washington. Version 1.0. Oregon and Washington. Oregon-Washington Partners in Flight. Online. (www.orwapif.org/pdf/western_forest.pdf). Accessed 4 March 2009.

Altman, B. 2000. Conservation strategy for landbirds of the east-slope of the Cascade Mountains in Oregon and Washington. Version 1.0. Oregon-Washington Partners in Flight. Online. (www.orwapif.org/pdf/east_slope.pdf). Accessed 4 March 2009.

California Department of Fish and Game (CDFG). 2005. California wildlife: Conservation challenges. (California's Wildlife Action Plan). Wildlife Health Center, University of California, Davis.

California Partners in Flight (CalPIF). 2002a. The draft coniferous forest bird conservation plan: A strategy for protecting and managing coniferous forest habitats and associated birds in California (J. Robinson and J. Alexander, lead authors). Version 1.0. Point Reyes Bird Observatory, Stinson Beach, CA. Online. (www.prbo.org/calpif/plans.html). Accessed 4 March 2009.

California Partners in Flight (CalPIF). 2002b. The oak woodland bird conservation plan: A strategy for protecting and managing oak woodland habitats and associated birds in California (S. Zack, lead author). Version 2.0. Online. (www.prbo.org/calpif/plans.html). Accessed 4 March 2009.

California Partners in Flight (CalPIF). 2004. The coastal scrub and chaparral bird conservation plan: A strategy for protecting and managing coastal scrub and chaparral habitats and associated birds in California (J. Lovio, lead author). Version 2.0. PRBO Conservation Science, Stinson Beach, CA. Online. (www.prbo.org/calpif/plans.html). Accessed 4 March 2009.

California Partners in Flight (CalPIF). 2005. The sagebrush bird conservation plan: A strategy for protecting and managing sagebrush habitats and associated birds in California. Version 1.0. PRBO Conservation Science, Stinson Beach, CA. Online. (www.prbo.org/calpif/plans.html). Accessed 4 March 2009.

DellaSala, D. A., S. B. Reid, T. J. Frest, J. R. Strittholt, and D. M. Olson. 1999. A global perspective on the biodiversity of the Klamath-Siskiyou Ecoregion. Natural Areas Journal 19:300-319.

Frey, R. I., J. L. Stephens, and J. D. Alexander. 2010. Summary report: Klamath Bird Observatory's 2009 long-term constant effort monitoring station efforts in the Klamath-Siskiyou Bioregion. Rep. No. KBO-2010-0002. Klamath Bird Observatory, Ashland, Oregon.

Oregon Department of Fish and Wildlife (ODFW). 2005. Oregon conservation strategy. Oregon Department of Fish and Wildlife, Salem, Oregon.

Ralph, C. J., G. R. Guepel, P. Pyle, T. E. Martin, and D. F. DeSante. 1993. Handbook of field methods for monitoring landbirds. USDA Forest Service General Technical Report PSW-GTR-144.

Riparian Habitat Joint Venture (RHJV). 2004. The riparian bird conservation plan: A strategy for reversing the decline of riparian associated birds in California. Version 2.0. California Partners in Flight. Online. (www.prbo.org/calpif/plans.html). Accessed 4 March 2009.

Rich, T. D., C. J. Beardmore, H. Berlanga, P. J. Blancher, M. S. W. Bradstreet, G. S. Butcher, D. W. Demarest, E. H. Dunn, W. C. Hunter, E. E. Iñigo-Elias, J. A. Kennedy, A. M. Martell, A. O. Panjabi, D. N. Pashley, K. V. Rosenberg, C. M. Rustay, J. S. Wendt, and T. C. Will. 2004. Partners in Flight North American landbird conservation plan. Cornell Lab of Ornithology, Ithaca, New York.

Sarr, D. A., D. C. Odion, S. R. Mohren, E. E. Perry, R. L. Hoffman, L. K. Bridy, and A. A. Merton. 2007. Vital signs monitoring plan for the Klamath Network: Phase III report. U.S. Department of the Interior, National Park Service Klamath Network Inventory and Monitoring Program. Ashland, Oregon. Natural Resource Technical Report NPS/KLMN/NRR--2007/016.

Stephens, J. L., and J. D. Alexander. 2010. Klamath Bird Observatory spring point counts and fall area searches: 2009 effort report. Rep. No. KBO-2010-0003. Klamath Bird Observatory, Ashland, Oregon.

Stephens, J. L., S. R. Mohren, J. D. Alexander, D. A. Sarr, and K. M. Irvine. 2010. Klamath Network landbird monitoring protocol. Natural Resource Report NPS/KLMN/NRR—2010/187. National Park Service, Fort Collins, Colorado.

Stevens, D. L., and A. R. Olsen. 2004. Spatially balanced sampling of natural resources. Journal of the American Statistical Association 99:262–278.

Trail, P. W., R. Cooper, and D. Vroman. 1997. The breeding birds of the Klamath/Siskiyou region. Pages 158-174 in J. J. Beigel, E. S. Jules, and B. Snitkin, editors. Proceedings of the first conference on Siskiyou ecology. Siskiyou Regional Education Project, Cave Junction, Oregon.

APPENDIX A

Sampling frames for each KLMN park unit as developed in the Klamath Network:Lanbird Monitoring Protocol.

National Park Service Klamath Network
Long-term Landbird Monitoring Sampling Frame
Crater Lake National Park

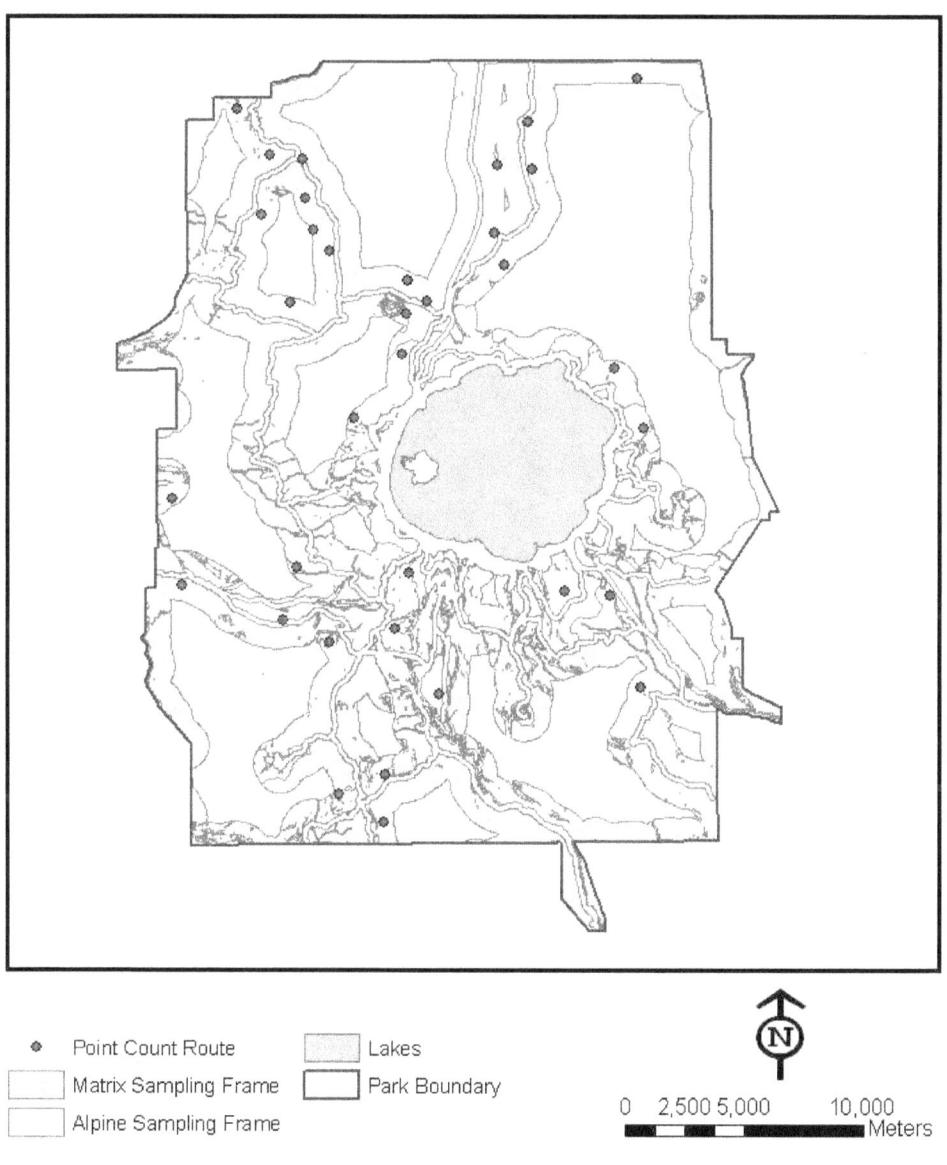

Figure 1. Alpine and matrix sampling frames at Crater Lake National Park.

National Park Service Klamath Network
Long-term Landbird Monitoring Sampling Frame
Lassen Volcanic National Park

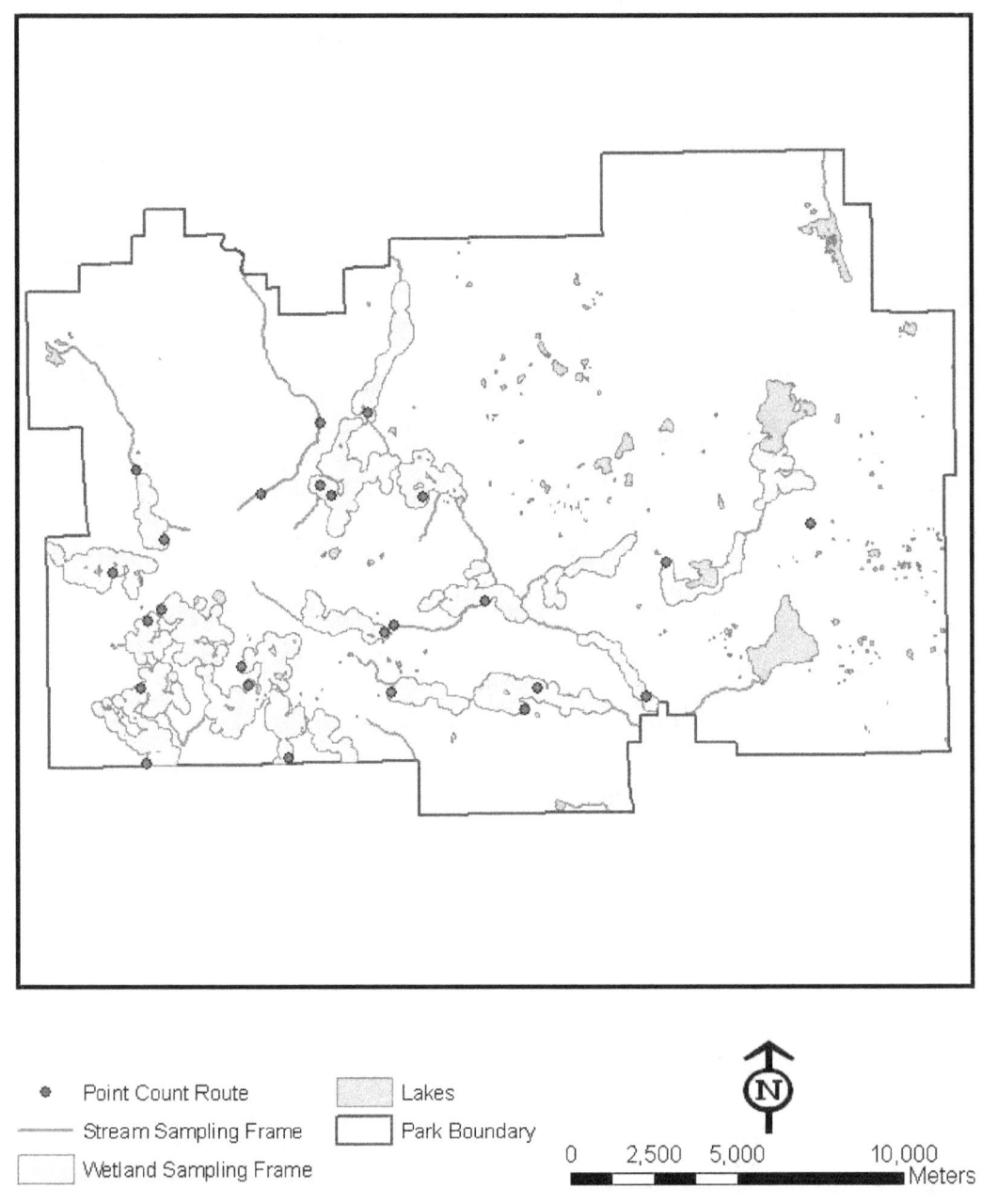

Point Count Route
Stream Sampling Frame
Wetland Sampling Frame
Lakes
Park Boundary

0 2,500 5,000 10,000 Meters

N

Figure 2. Riparian sampling frame at Lassen Volcanic National Park.

National Park Service Klamath Network
Long-term Landbird Monitoring Sampling Frame
Lava Beds National Monument

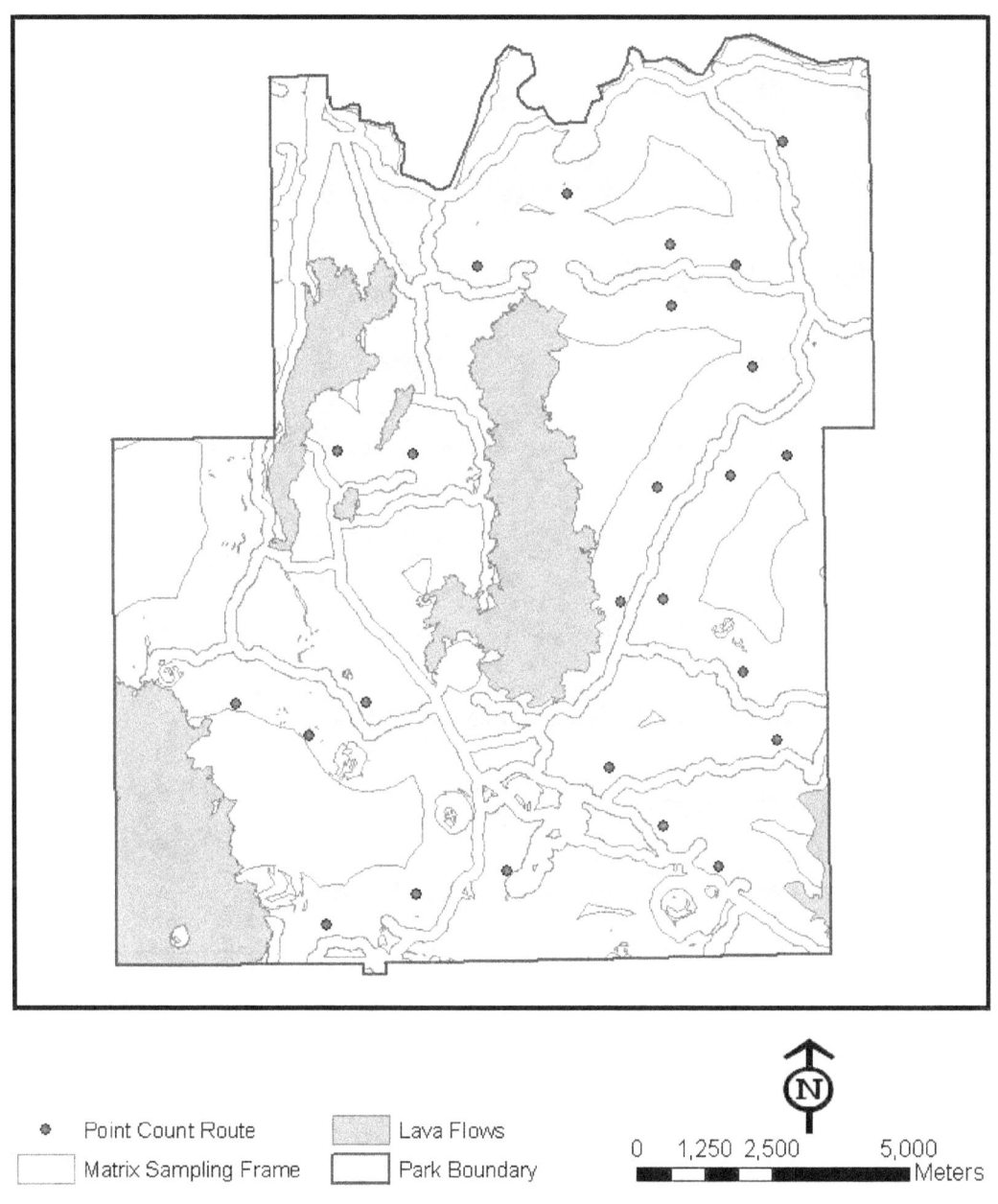

Point Count Route
Matrix Sampling Frame
Lava Flows
Park Boundary

0   1,250 2,500   5,000
Meters

N

Figure 3. Matrix sampling frame at Lava Beds National Monument.

National Park Service Klamath Network
Long-term Landbird Monitoring Sampling Frame
Oregon Caves National Monument

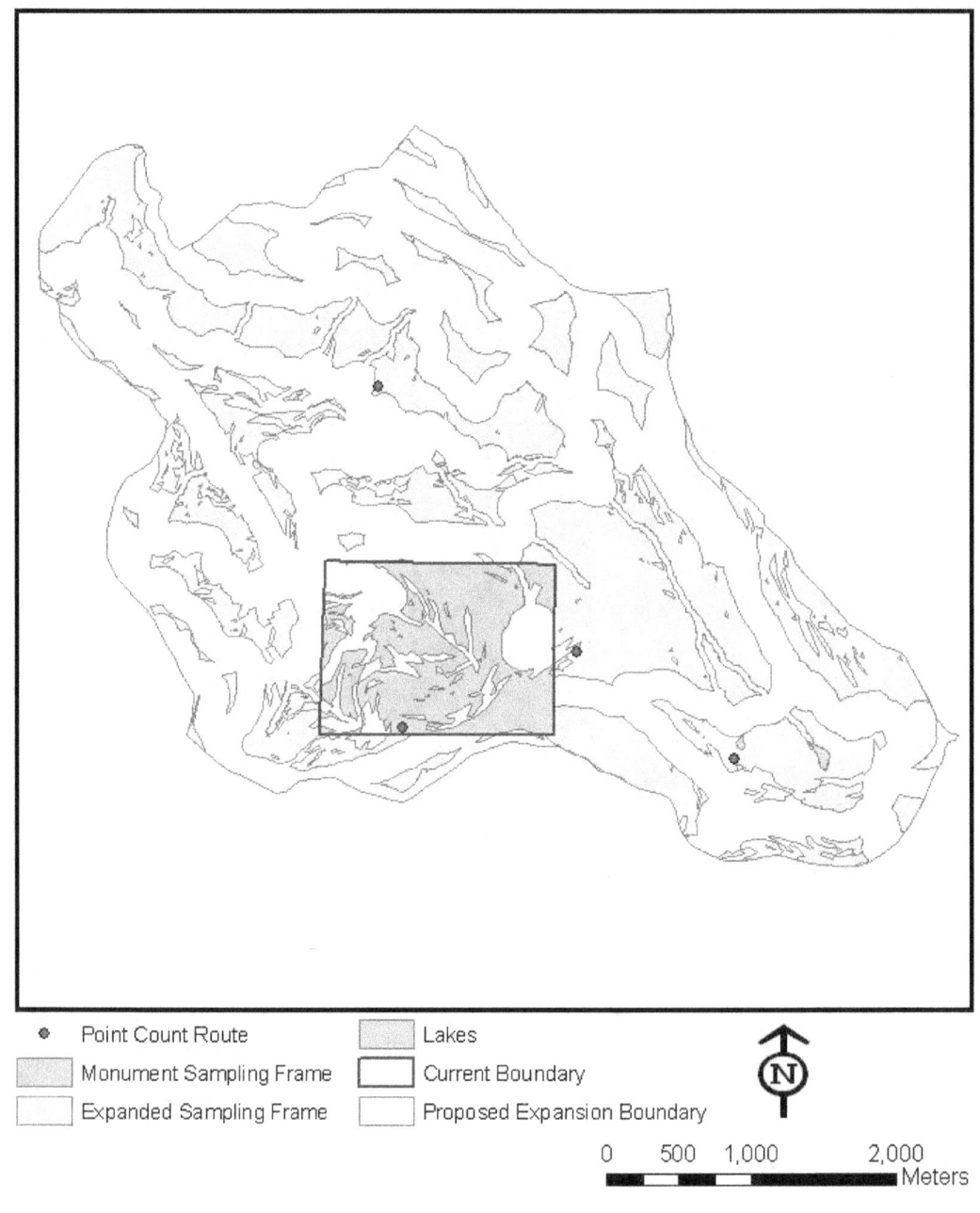

● Point Count Route	▨ Lakes
▨ Monument Sampling Frame	☐ Current Boundary
☐ Expanded Sampling Frame	☐ Proposed Expansion Boundary

0   500   1,000   2,000
Meters

Figure 4. Matrix sampling frame at Oregon Caves National Monument.

National Park Service Klamath Network
Long-term Landbird Monitoring Sampling Frame
Redwood National and State Parks North Overview

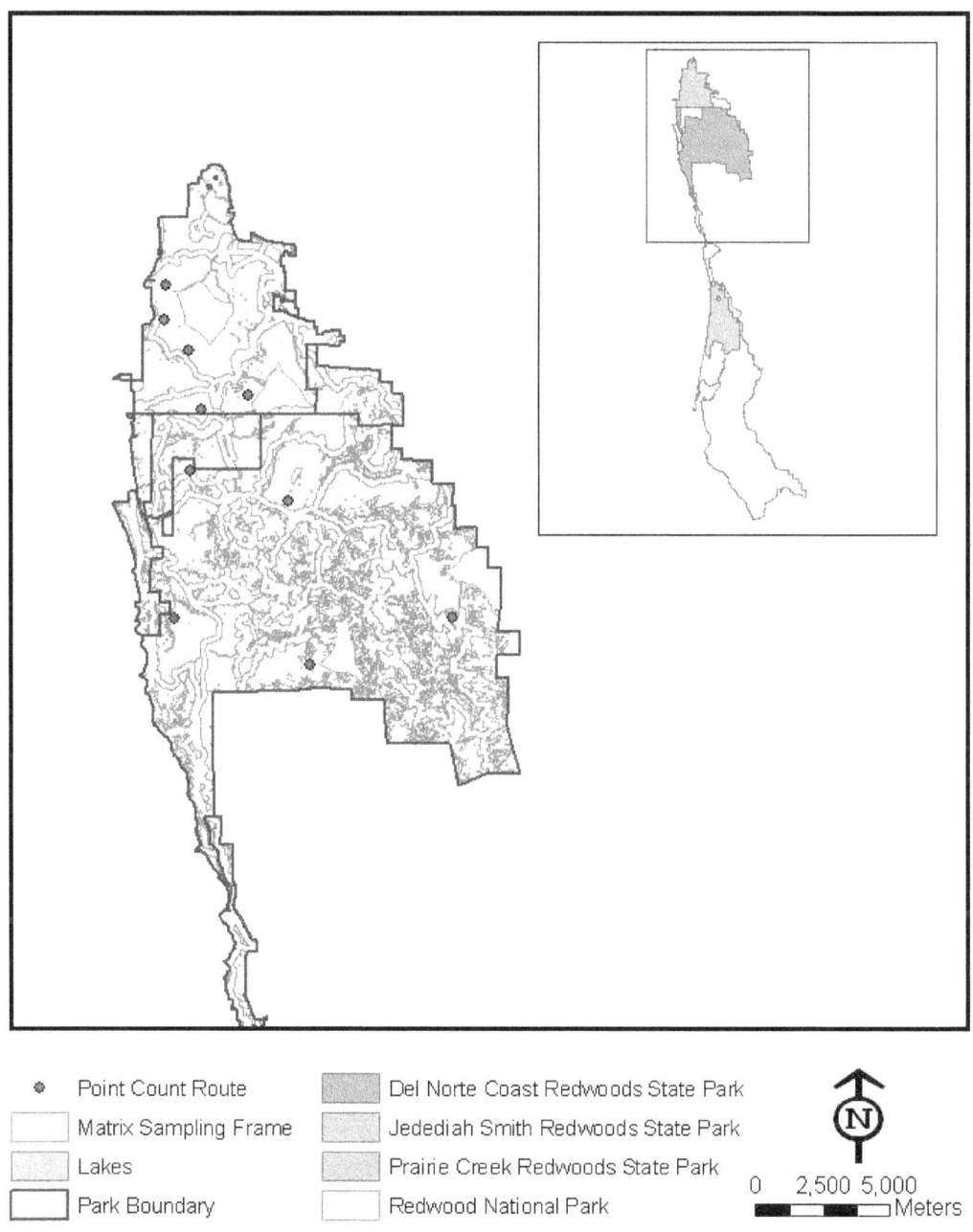

● Point Count Route	Del Norte Coast Redwoods State Park	
Matrix Sampling Frame	Jedediah Smith Redwoods State Park	
Lakes	Prairie Creek Redwoods State Park	
Park Boundary	Redwood National Park	0 2,500 5,000 Meters

Figure 5. Northern portion of Matrix sampling frame at Redwood National and State Parks.

National Park Service Klamath Network
Long-term Landbird Monitoring Sampling Frame
Redwood National and State Parks South Overview

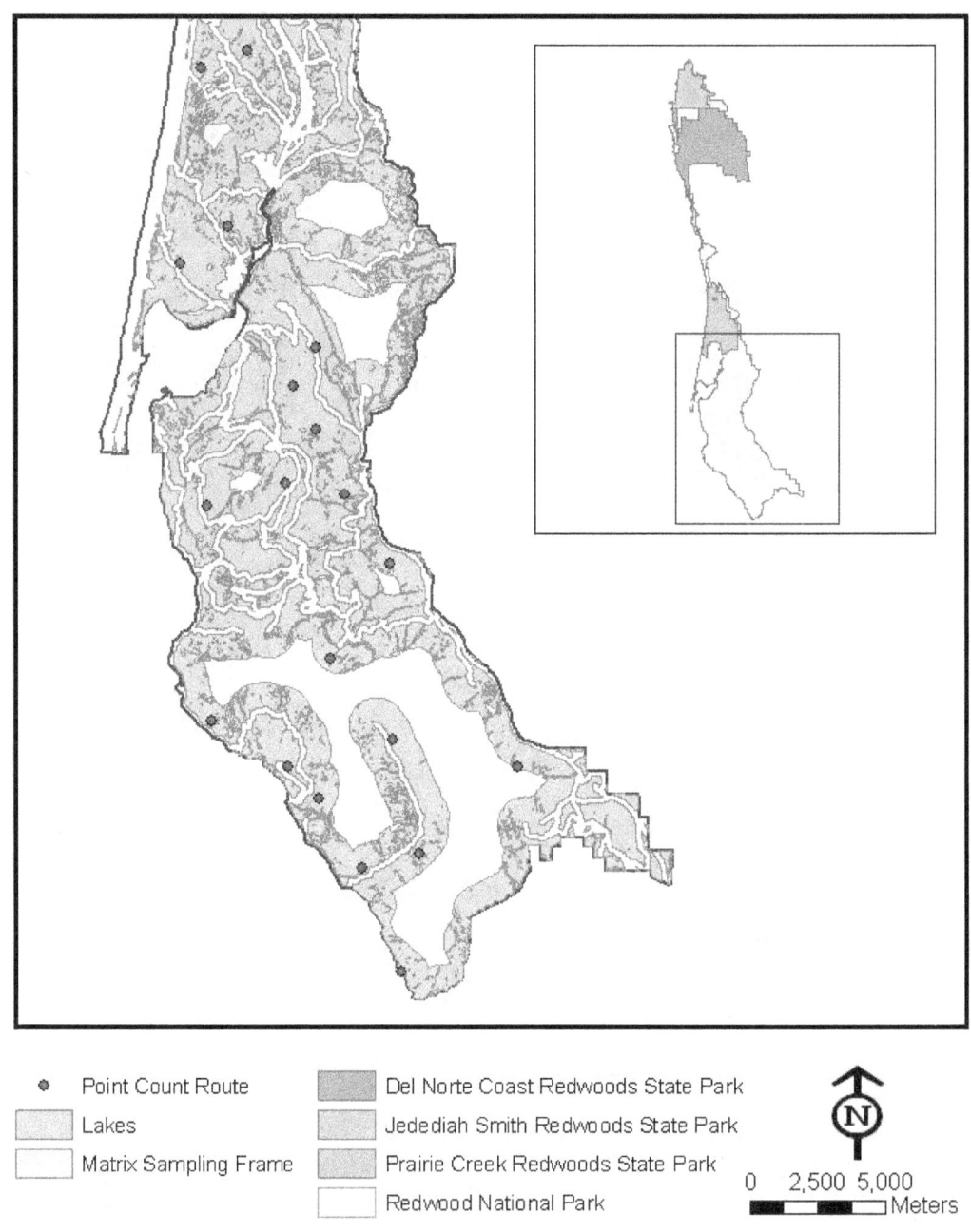

● Point Count Route

▨ Lakes

☐ Matrix Sampling Frame

▨ Del Norte Coast Redwoods State Park

▨ Jedediah Smith Redwoods State Park

▨ Prairie Creek Redwoods State Park

☐ Redwood National Park

N

0   2,500 5,000
Meters

Figure 6. Southern portion of Matrix sampling frame at Redwood National and State Parks.

National Park Service Klamath Network
Long-term Landbird Monitoring Sampling Frame
Whiskeytown National Monument

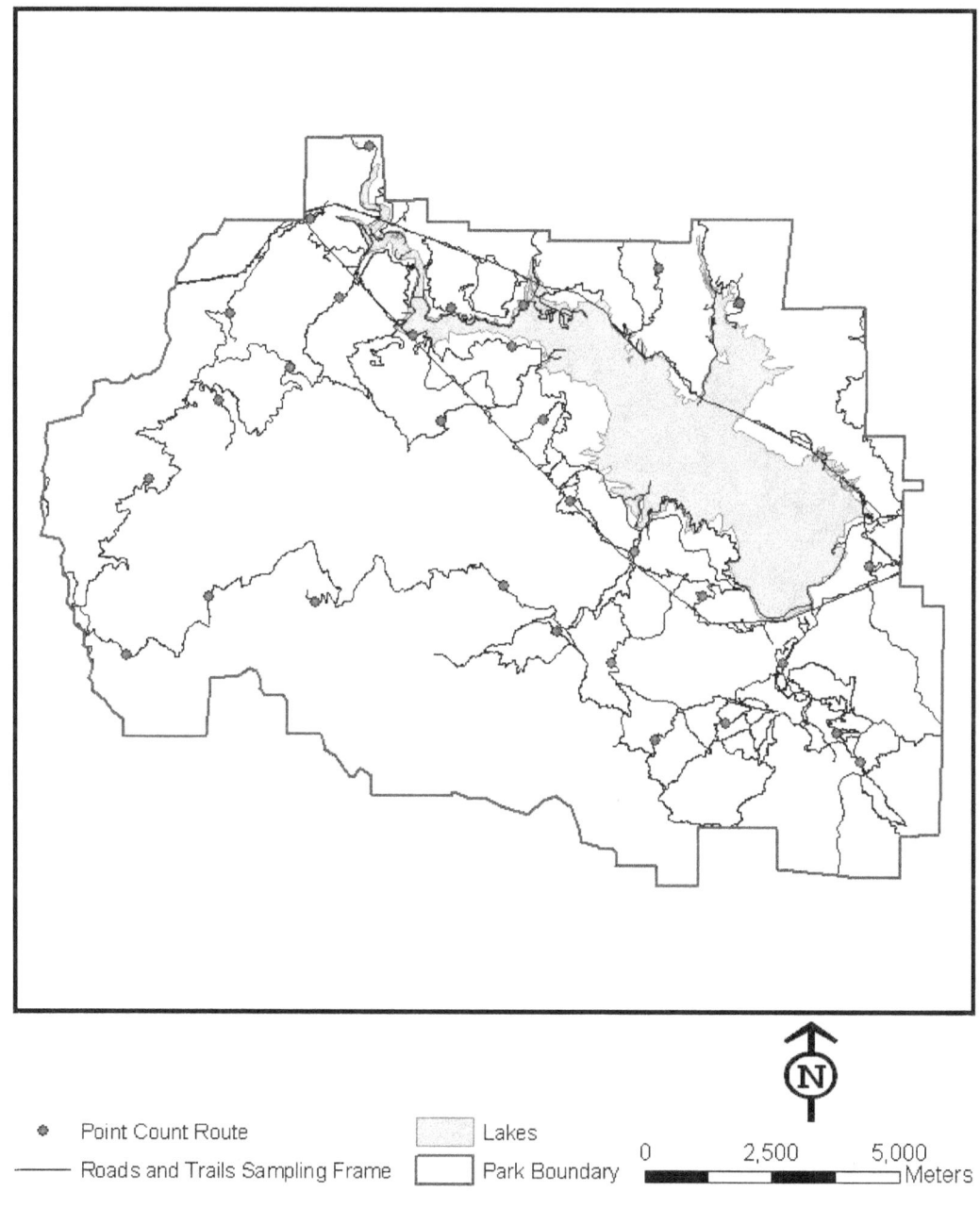

• Point Count Route	Lakes
—— Roads and Trails Sampling Frame	Park Boundary

0   2,500   5,000
Meters

Figure 7. The sampling frame at Whiskeytown National Recreation Area was limited to roads, trails, and powerlines.

APPENDIX B

Klamath Network Landbird Monitoring Protocol:
Rules for designating landbird point count routes in ArcGIS

Jaime L. Stephens

For choosing VCP sampling locations, we used an algorithm termed the Generalized Random Tessellation Stratified (GRTS) method to develop spatially balanced sampling locations within each selected sampling frame for each Park. To establish a systematic random sampling route around each GRTS sample, 11 adjacent sites are placed 250 m apart, according to a set of rules. These rules ensure that a grid is set up as closely around the GRTS sample as possible, using a systematic, random approach within constraints of the defined sampling frame. Depending on the sampling frame, the routes are established either in a block (matrix, alpine, wetland) or line (roads, streams).

For non-linear routes (CRLA, LABE, ORCA, RNSP):

1) Grids were built in ArcGIS placing sites 250 m apart within a 1000 m radius on cardinal direction orientation, using Hawths Tools conditional point sampling tools. This provided plenty of potential sites (47 sites) to accommodate the selection process detailed below.

    a. If the GRTS sample is less than 125 m from the Park edge, then the GRTS sample will be dropped and replaced with the next GRTS sample within the same time series.
    b. While following the subsequent rule set, if any site along a route is less than 250 m from a previously established site it will not be included.
    c. If a site is less than 125 m from the Park edge it will not be included.
    d. Each route must be established within a contiguous piece of sampling frame (e.g. it can not cross a road) for CRLA, LABE, LAVO, and RNSP. This rule could not be met for ORCA.
    e. For any given route, the situation where the extra distance traveled between sites (to travel around an area that is not included in the sampling frame, e.g. lava field) cannot exceed 350 m total.
    f. If greater than 1/6 of the interior of the route is non-sampling frame (i.e. lava field), then the GRTS sample will be dropped and replaced with the next GRTS sample within the same time series.

2) From these grid sites, build a block of eight sites around the GRTS sample, with the GRTS sample in the center.

3) If not possible, role a dice to choose a random direction in which to build a block of eight sites with the GRTS sample in the center of one edge.

4) If not possible, role a dice to choose a random direction in which to build a block of eight sites with the GRTS sample in the corner of the block.

5) If not possible to fit an entire 8 site block, build as much of it as possible using steps 2-4. Afterwards, refer to the next step for placing remaining sites.

    a. If the establishment of the initial block is limited by a previously established route, the GRTS sample will be dropped and replaced with the next GRTS sample from the same time series.

6) Place remaining sites (for a total of 12 sites and an extra 3 sites as oversamples) in sets of 3 around and adjacent to the grid, rolling a dice for a random direction until all sites are placed.

7) If sets of 3 do not fit around grid, repeat rolling dice for random direction, for sets of 2 sites until all sites are placed.

8) If sets of 2 do not fit around the grid, repeat rolling dice for random direction, for 1 site at a time until all sites are placed.

9) If no more sites fit around the gird, choose sites in a random direction by sets of 3, then 2, then 1.

10) If the above criteria can not be met, and thus 12 sites (and 3 oversamples) can not be fit contiguously within a block of the sampling frame, the GRTS sample will be dropped and replaced with the next GRTS sample within the same time series.

For linear routes (LAVO stream sampling frame, WHIS):

1. Eleven sites are placed 250 m apart in both directions from the GRTS sample to form a route.

    a. If the GRTS sample is less than 125 m from the Park edge, then the GRTS sample will be dropped and replaced with the next GRTS sample within the same time series.
    b. While following the subsequent rule set, if any site along a route is less than 250 m from a previously established site it will not be included.
    c. If a site is less than 125 m from the Park edge it will not be included.
    d. For any given route, an extra 1000 m of road or trail distance between one site and the next is allowable. If this is exceeded, add sites to the road/trail in the other direction as needed. For any given route, an extra 350 m of stream distance

between one site and the next is allowable. If this is exceeded, add sites to the stream in the other direction as needed.

2. If there are not road/trail/stream junctions, build a route with an equal amount of sites on each side of the GRTS sample. Roll a die to determine which end of the route to add the last site to.

    a. If you cannot place a site due to proximity of a previously established route, continue along that road/trail/stream in the same direction until you reach the first possible place to put a site.
    b. If you cannot place a site due to proximity to the Park boundary, add sites to the road/trail/stream in the other direction as needed.

3. If there are road/trail/stream junctions encountered when designating the route, lay out the sites as indicated in step 2 until you reach an intersection. At the intersection, role a dice to choose a random direction to indicate which road/trail/stream the route will continue on.

4. If the road/trail/stream ends or you exceed the allowable extra travel distance, trace back to either:
    a. The first intersection you encounter going backwards and add remaining sites or
    b. If you do not encounter an intersection, add sites to the end in the opposite direction from the GRTS sample.

APPENDIX C

Location of point count routes for each KLMN park unit as developed in the Klamath Network:Lanbird Monitoring Protocol.

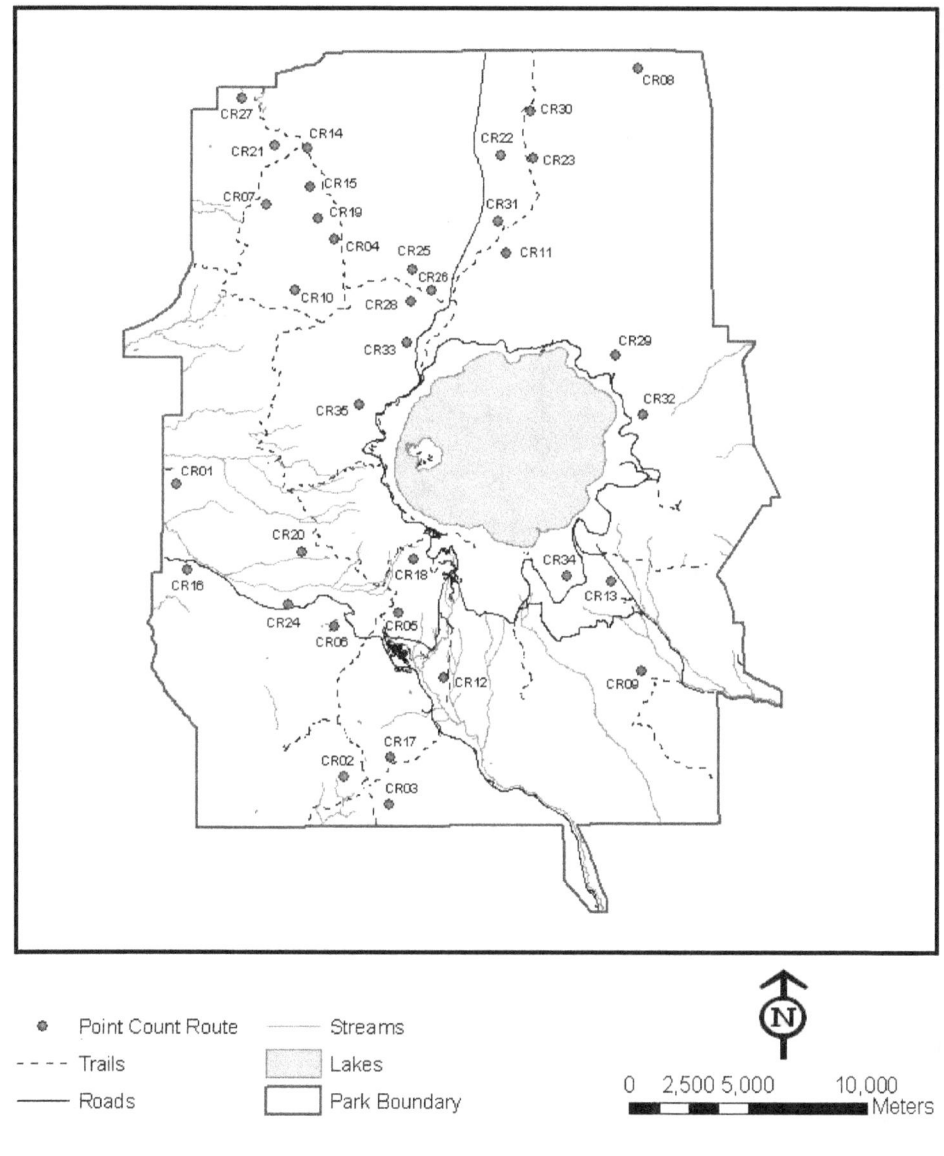

Figure 1. Location of point count routes at Crater Lake National Park.

National Park Service Klamath Network
Long-term Landbird Monitoring Routes
Lassen Volcanic National Park

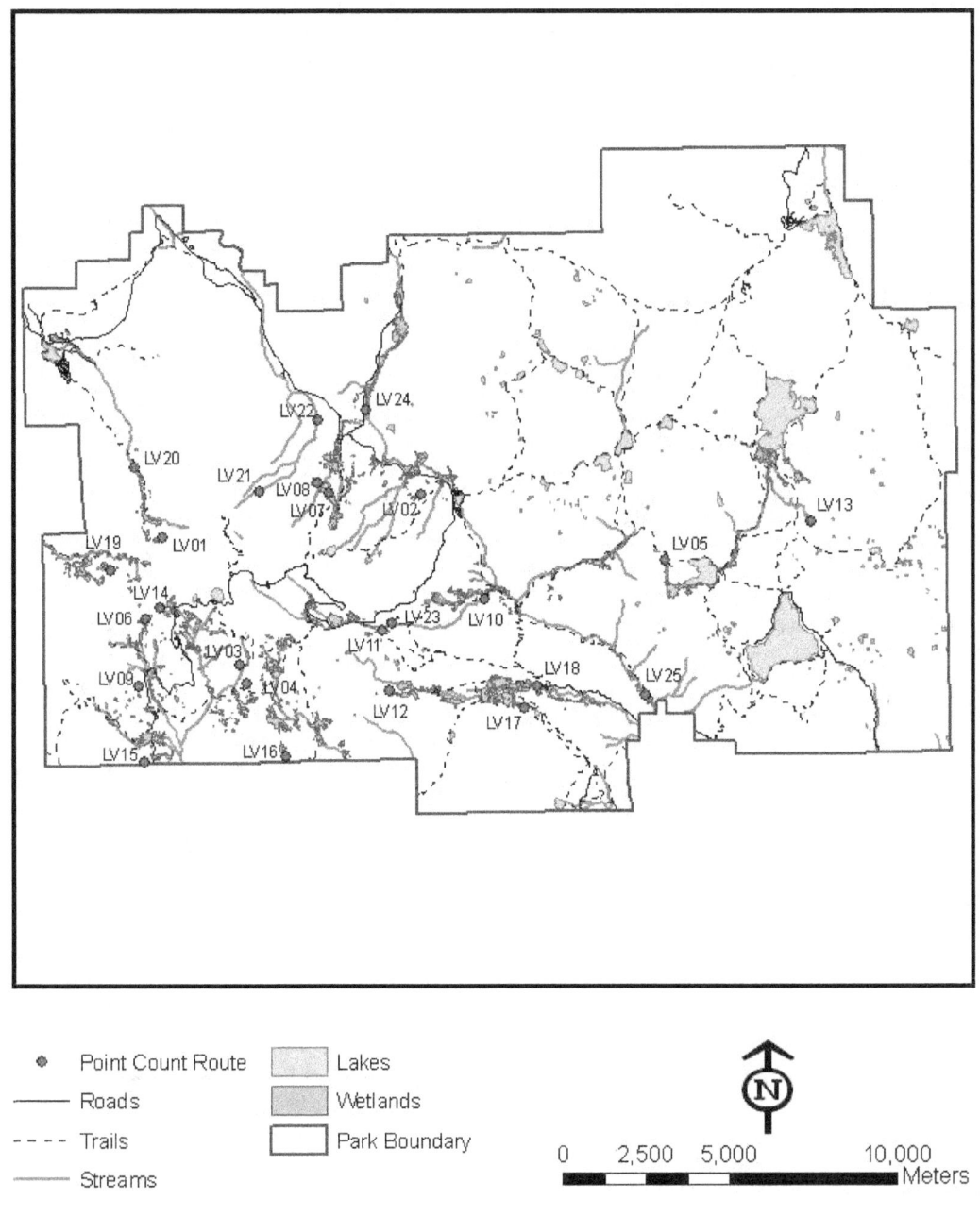

Figure 2. Location of point count routes at Lassen Volcanic National Park.

National Park Service Klamath Network
Long-term Landbird Monitoring Routes
Lava Beds National Monument

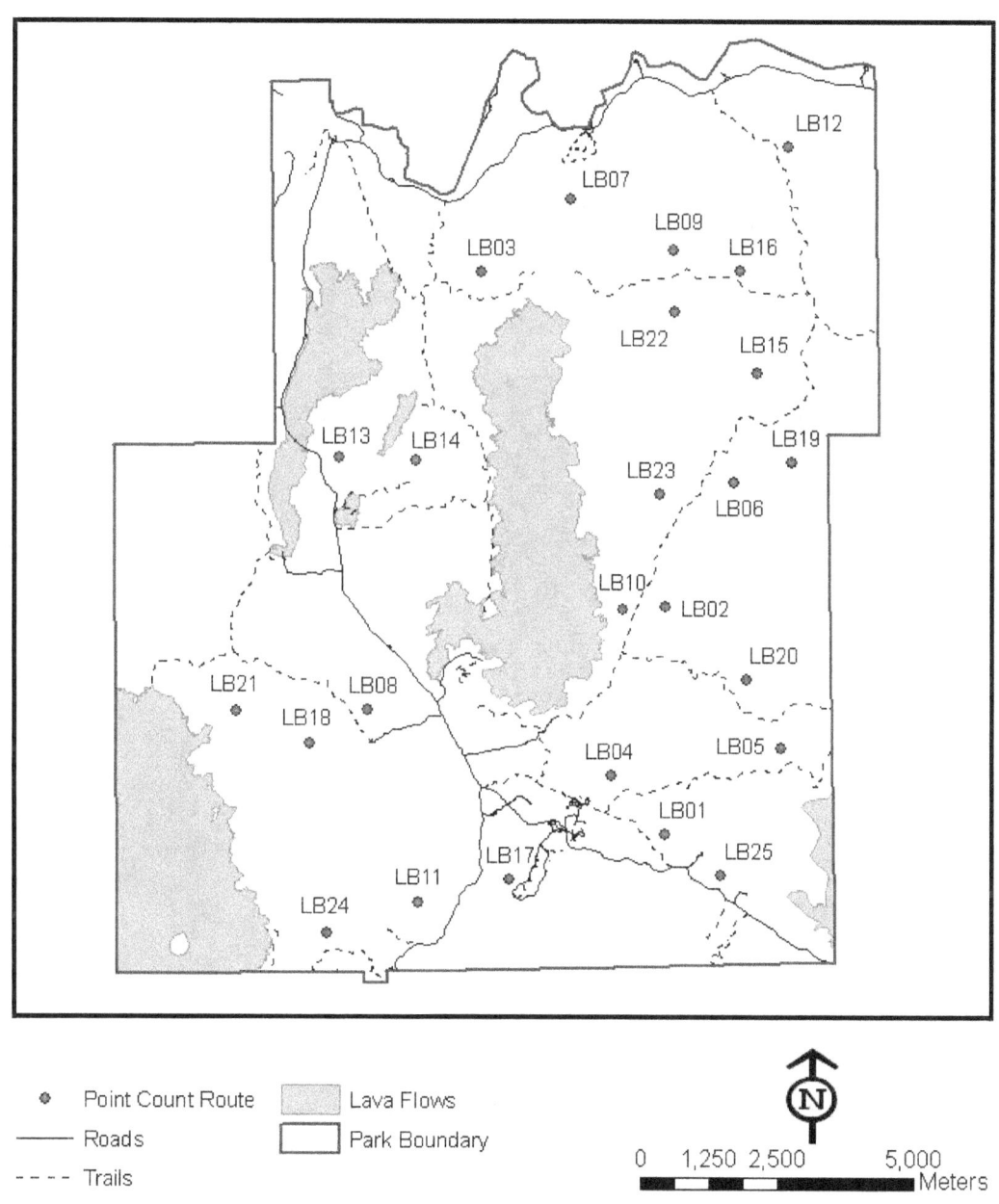

Figure 3. Location of point count routes at at Lava Beds National Monument.

National Park Service Klamath Network
Long-term Landbird Monitoring Routes
Oregon Caves National Monument

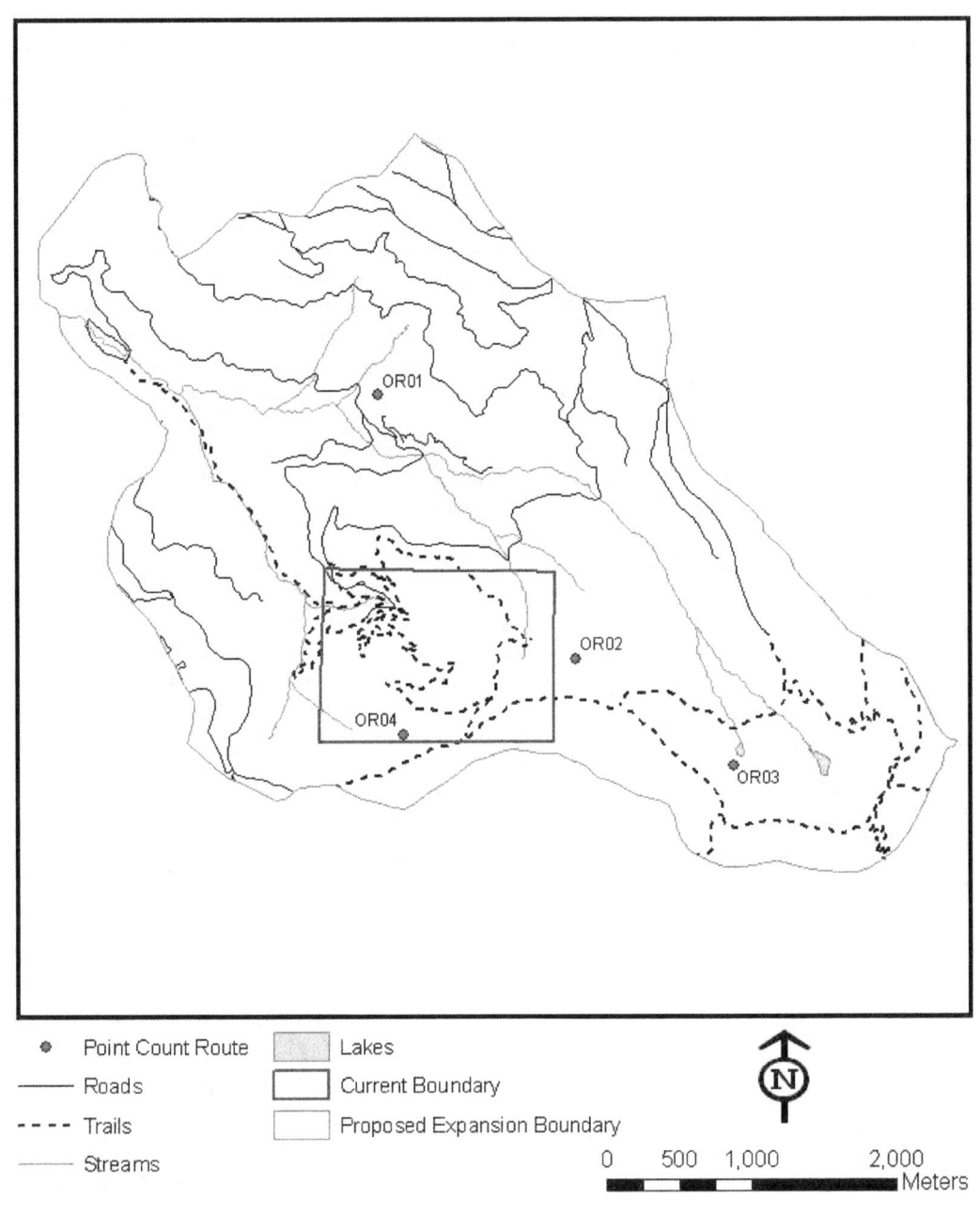

Figure 4. Location of point count routes at Oregon Caves National Monument.

National Park Service Klamath Network
Long-term Landbird Monitoring Routes
Redwood National and State Parks North Overview

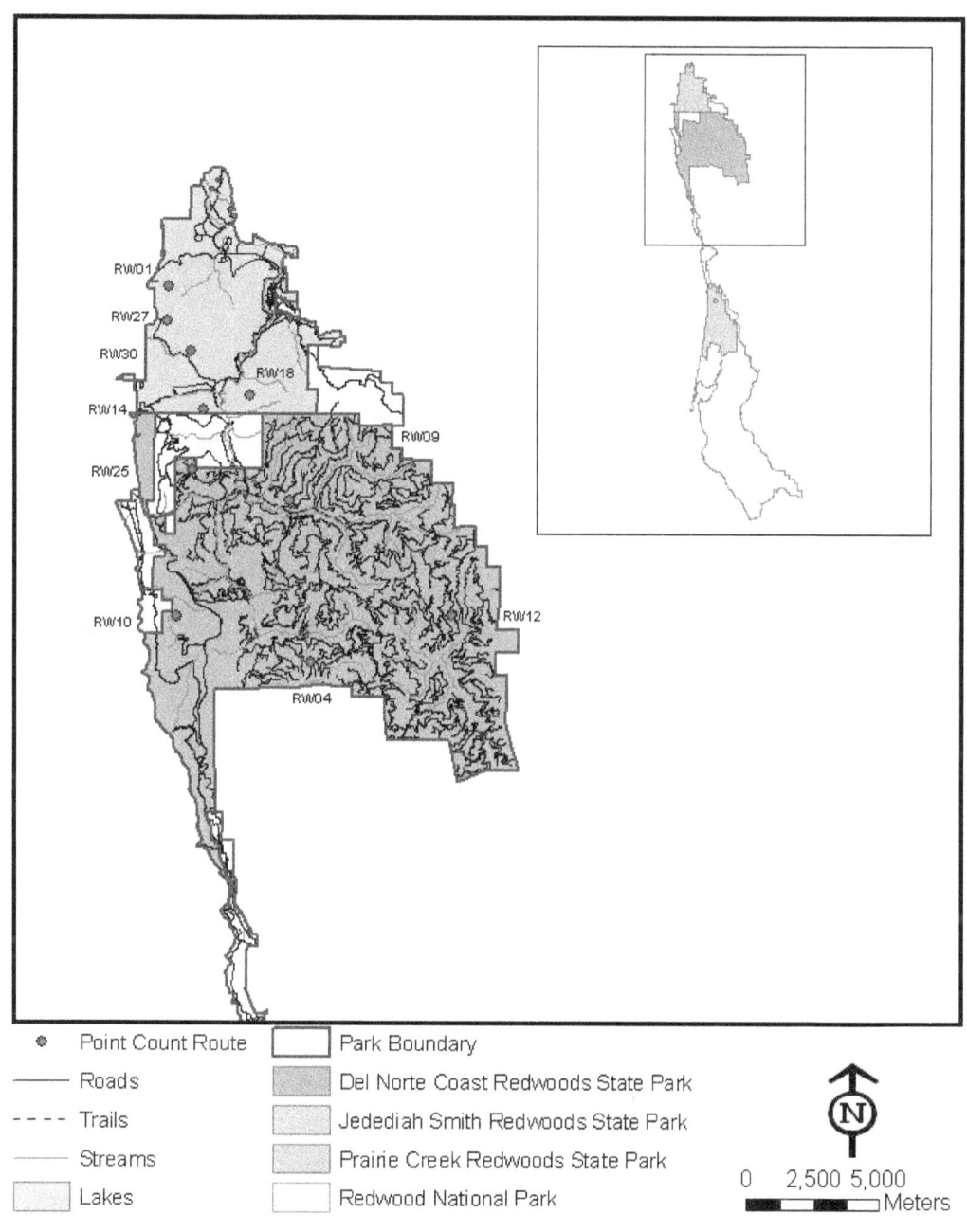

	Point Count Route		Park Boundary
——	Roads		Del Norte Coast Redwoods State Park
- - - -	Trails		Jedediah Smith Redwoods State Park
——	Streams		Prairie Creek Redwoods State Park
	Lakes		Redwood National Park

0   2,500   5,000 Meters

Figure 5. Location of point count routes in the northern portion of Redwood National and State Parks.

National Park Service Klamath Network
Long-term Landbird Monitoring Routes
Redwood National and State Parks South Overview

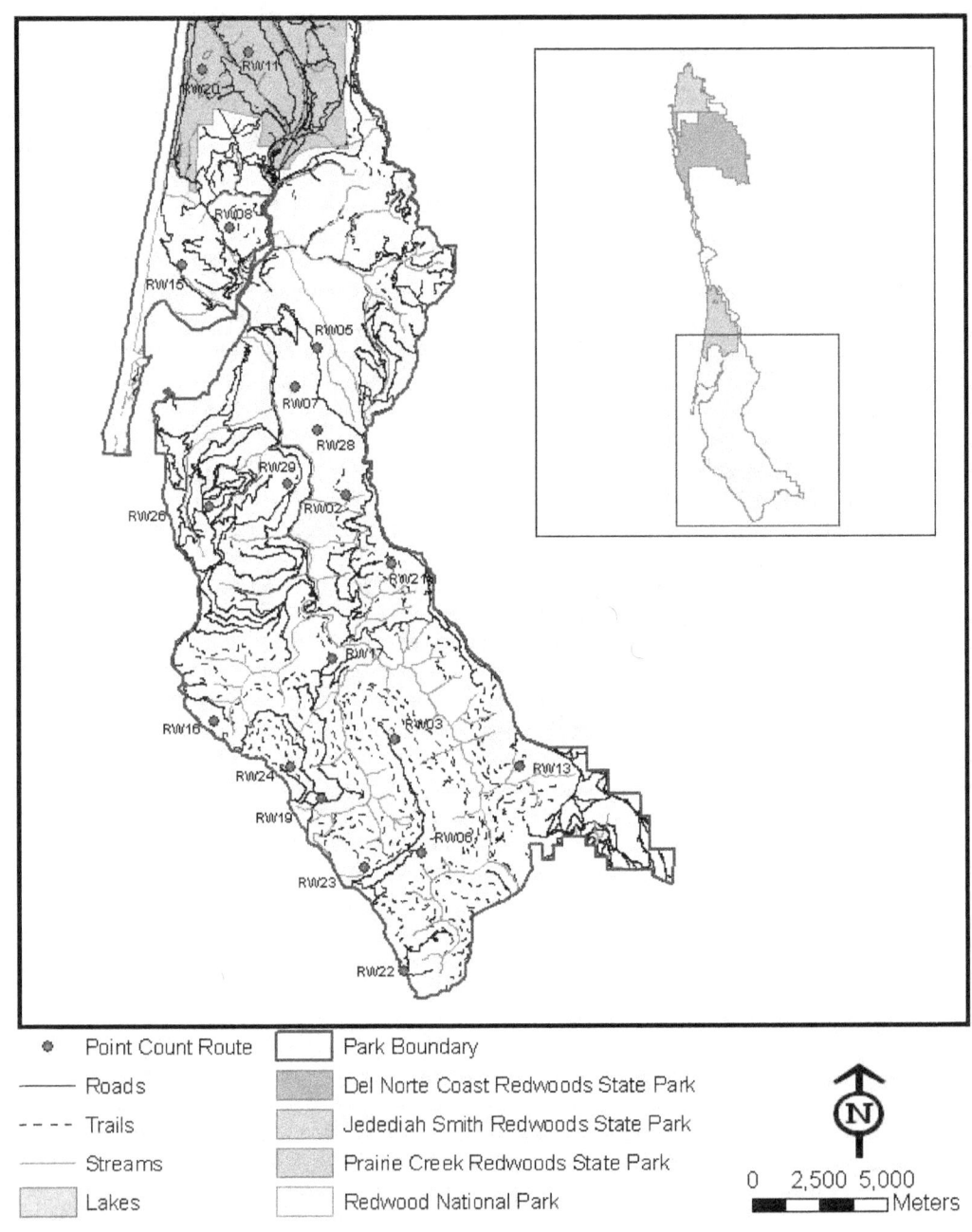

Figure 6. Location of point count routes in the southern portion of Redwood National and State Parks.

National Park Service Klamath Network
Long-term Landbird Monitoring Routes
Whiskeytown National Monument

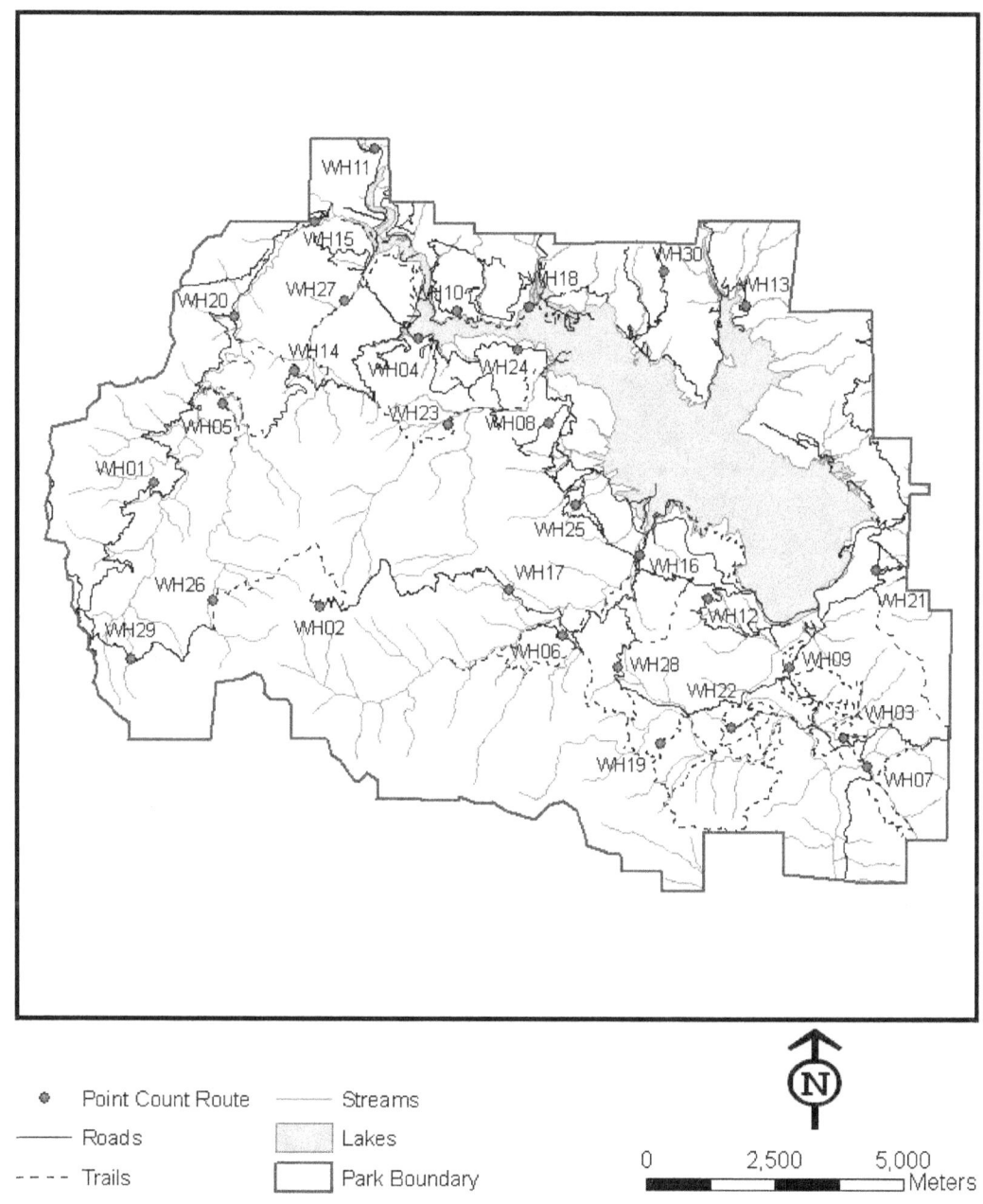

Figure 7. Location of point count routes at Whiskeytown National Recreation Area.

www.ingramcontent.com/pod-product-compliance
Lightning Source LLC
Chambersburg PA
CBHW080931290526
45795CB00007BA/2705